MW00628969

Be great!

The 9-5 Entrepreneur
Twelve Questions to Consider Before Taking the LEAP

Cover Design, Book Layout and Interior Design: Enger Lanier Taylor for In Due Season Publishing

Contributing Editor: Dwaynia Wilkerson - Prose & Pens

Published By: In Due Season Publishing
Huntsville, Alabama 35810
indueseasonpublishing@gmail.com
www.indueseasonpublishing.com

ISBN-13: 978-0-9992387-3-8
ISBN-10: 0999238736

PREFACE

In 2008, while phenomenal educators in the making, we started Holt & Holt Entrepreneurship in Huntsville, Alabama as a residential and commercial lawn care business. We were due to be married in less than three months, and knowing that Huntsville would be our home and was an established city with endless opportunities, we knew that establishing Holt & Holt Entrepreneurship would be beneficial. We were excited about our life together and our business. As with most new businesses, our first contracts came from family, friends and their referrals. Landing commercial contracts called for us to be more intentional and aggressive in our efforts. We did not mind because we set out to be among the best in our area, and we were willing to put in the work to make sure it happened.

One of our best attributes, and one that we know set us apart from others, was our commitment to providing quality service regardless of how big or small the job. Even at the start of our business, whether we were being paid twenty-five dollars or one hundred dollars, we provided the same level of service. We understood that quality over quantity was the only way to ensure that our clients continued to remain loyal.

While we were gaining more and more traction around town, the 2008 economic recession was in full force. It was on a steady decline and people's financial lives were crumbling. The government and banks were being blamed; businesses were closing; jobs were being lost; and dream homes were being foreclosed. In the midst of it all, we were introduced to a new concept and opportunity to expand our business. Because foreclosed properties were going back to their respective lending institutions, they were often left abandoned and damaged or became a gathering spot for squatters. The properties needed to be cleaned, rehabilitated and preserved. That is where we would come in with property preservation. Property preservation allowed us to add an entirely new and unprecedented dimension to our business. It also brought us adventures and experiences, some good and others not so much. Nevertheless, it was the start of us not only being among the best businesses in our area, but we became leaders and game changers.

The best lesson that we learned from the economic recession was that times of hardship call for ingenuity. People rarely mention that in order to succeed at entrepreneurship, you have to be willing and eager to learn. Fear of the unknown or something new will only limit your ability to capitalize and grow. Property preservation was new to us, and we spent so many hours learning, researching, and reading about the industry that we lost count. After creating lesson plans for the next day, we would spend the rest of our time on Google learning this new industry to which we had been introduced. We found it exciting to read about other business owners who had been successful in this industry, which ignited an even stronger flame to learn.

Today, we are proud to say that we have become leaders in our industry. Not only have we grown and expanded, but we have helped our team members to grow and expand as well. Some of our contractors have broadened their scope of services. Others have gone on to start their own businesses as a result of what they've experienced and learned under our helm. Though we had some great successes, those things did not come without our share of losses. We lost friends, family members became distant, we have parted ways with business partners, and we have experienced some personal setbacks, but through all of that, we have remained strong and are happy to be able to share our story with you.

Entrepreneurs in the Making

Martell

If I had to name one thing I have always known, it is that you have to work hard and possess a strong sense of ambition. I have literally been working hard my entire life. Thinking back, I would say that I had my first stint at entrepreneurship in the third grade. I was that ambitious kid in the neighborhood knocking on your door to mow your lawn and rake your leaves. By the fourth grade, I had actually built a clientele of neighbors who were all too willing to allow my sometimes awkward skills to grace the fronts of their homes. Fall became my favorite season because freshly fallen leaves meant another opportunity for me to increase my services. It should not have come as a surprise to anyone who truly knew me that my entrepreneurial start as an adult came in the form of lawn care.

What actually may have been surprising was that I had any entrepreneurial spirit at all. You see, my upbringing is the familiar tale of a young black male raised by a single mother. When I was three, my father was sentenced to nineteen years in prison. We had very little contact during his incarceration, but oddly enough he was still a great teacher even in his absence. I learned at a young age that doing wrong would land you nowhere really quickly, or it would land you in prison. I tried my best to stay away from trouble because I did not want to end up in a similar situation as my father. Trouble, however, is easy to find, even in a small city. With little direction and no real father figure, my life could have ended up very differently.

However, I had my mother, and she was my saving grace. My mother did not graduate from high school and never went on to get her GED. She was, however, an extremely hard worker. Although we were poor, I never knew it until others brought it my attention. We did not have tons of money, but my younger brother and I never really noticed. She always made sure that we were well fed and clothed. Of course, we did not have the designer clothing that some of the kids wore, but there were many kids in our neighborhood who were just enough like us that we did not feel like outsiders. She spent quality time with us doing things that did not require a lot of money. When she did have extra money and wanted to treat us, we would splurge at Chuck E Cheese's.

Although my mom did not go to church often, she always made sure I went. I am still not sure how I ended up on that church bus that traveled from a predominately white neighborhood across town to a predominantly black neighborhood and back again. Inside the Baptist church, I would get into trouble for the exact things I did at school. I was a talker and a socializer and regardless of the environment, I wanted to talk and socialize. Nevertheless, I would be invited back Sunday after Sunday, and each time I would return.

Because my mom was such a hard worker, I do not see any way that trait could have bypassed me. The belief that I need to do whatever is necessary to provide for my family was definitely a result of my mother's example. I remember her working fast food jobs at Wendy's and Hardees. I remember walks to the local grocery store and hauling the bags back home. I also remember our first car. It was called a "hoopty" back in the day. She bought it for only five hundred dollars, but you would have thought she pulled up in a Rolls Royce when she brought it home. During those times when she could have cursed my father and walked away from her responsibilities, she never did and she never complained. She was always positive, even in the face of adversity.

Thankfully, by the time I entered high school, I found a love for ROTC and football. Both activities were game changers, and probably lifesavers, for me. They provided me with discipline and structure. I learned patience, leadership, and most importantly, how to be a team player. I took all of the skills I learned and channeled them into refining myself personally and in the eyes of my peers. I was no longer subjected to bullying or ridicule, but instead found that I was a natural leader. That realization, coupled with the influence of my Uncle Dexter, led me to college. He was the first in my family to ever graduate from college and I was the second. My primary reason for going to college was that I did not know what else to do. The next logical step after high school was college. I still had entrepreneurial ambition, but college would be something to fall back on if things got difficult. Once I decided to go to college, I also decided to become a teacher. It was no secret that I loved kids, so a major in special education was not farfetched.

During college, I played football and kept my grades up well enough to remain active on the team. Aside from my time on the field, I managed to work towards building my portfolio as an entrepreneur and continued to build a clientele. As a college student, I landed my first contract cleaning a local salon, and another contract with a dentist office followed. It was also during college that I met my soon to be wife and business partner, Melody.

After graduating college with a Bachelor of Arts in Special Education, I began teaching at a middle school. What I loved most about teaching was the kids and being able to coach. I got to spend the majority of my day doing two of the things I loved most. Oddly enough, I still felt out of place in the classroom.

Although I enjoyed teaching and coaching, the business was growing and I was starting to focus less on teaching and more on business. My colleagues began to notice too. Between answering calls, responding to clients and potential clients, and handling issues with employees, I was spending the better part of my day on the phone. Those around me started to complain, so I had to make a decision. Either I would stay in my teaching position and risk being fired, or I would need to exit the classroom and solely focus on tending to the needs of the business. After a year and a half of teaching, I decided to walk away. The profits from our lawn care business far exceeded my teaching salary and the business was commanding more and more of my attention. In hindsight, I know I made the right decision and the timing was perfect.

Melody

I was the quintessential overachiever. Despite growing up in a single parent home, my mother worked to ensure that I was actively involved in my church, my community and my school. She was training me to be a leader, to persevere, and to not allow circumstances to define my destiny. If something was happening in my hometown, there was a good chance I was involved, and leading. I had my first taste of performing at the age of five when I was asked to sing on television during the annual Christmas telethon. From there, I was hooked and began competing in pageants. I was a natural at pageants and went on to win the coveted title of Miss Brundidge. While I was thrilled to have won, I was most proud of making history as the first black Miss Brundidge, Alabama.

When it came to my community and my school, I was always eager to be involved and most of my family was eager to support me. I excelled in and outside of the classroom. I was the Student Government Association president, and president of 4-H and Future Business Leaders of America. I co-hosted a local gospel show and performed as a member of the gospel-recording group, Robert Lee Jr. and Friends. I got a thrill from performing, and every new opportunity helped me to be better than the last. As the end of high school neared, I had difficulty settling on a college major or a potential career path. During my early school years, I wanted to be a choreographer, a model, a lawyer, a singer, and sometimes I even wanted to be a teacher. I suppose that is how my high school English teacher was able to make such an impact on me. I admired the way she cared for her students and presented teaching as such a noble profession. I absolutely loved writing and editing, learning about subject-verb agreement and all of the aspects of the English language, so I followed her lead.

My time in college was just as mired in academics as high school. While most of my peers were partying and hanging around campus and local nightclubs, I was writing my next best paper, getting to know my professors, and making post college plans. Nevertheless, it was not necessarily all business. I did pledge a sorority and join a few student organizations.

In addition to studying like a mad woman, I managed to hold down a few jobs so that I would have spending money. Because I was well liked on campus, I was able to score a cushy job in the English department office answering phones and making copies for the professors, but I spent such a small amount of time fulfilling those job duties that I was able to maximize hours and use them as additional study time. On the weekends, I also worked as a leasing agent at a local apartment complex. Again, because of my work ethic and likability, I found favor with the apartment manager. As long as I did what was expected, I was able to focus on school and graduating. I also had a new love interest who was consuming a bit more of my time than I was accustomed. That love interest became my husband, Martell. He proposed to me the day I graduated college, and we have been inseparable since.

I started my teaching career as we were starting our lawn care business. Like Martell, I loved being in the classroom. Although my class always performed well, especially during testing, the administrative work took away from my love of teaching. I grew weary of the politics, internal conflicts, and administrative impositions. Because the business was doing so well, Martell continuously reminded me that I did not have to continue teaching. I was hoping that I would be able to make it through the school year, but the constant barrage of paperwork and the increased demand on classroom teachers became too much. I was over it. I left in the middle of a week in April. It may not have been the optimal exit, but it was necessary if I cared to maintain my sanity. Testing was over, so I did feel a sense of completion in spite of the fact that the school year had not technically ended. I honestly did not know, when I departed for school that morning, that it would be the last day I would teach middle school English.

QUESTIONS

QUESTION # 1
How do I know I am an entrepreneur?

To state it plainly, if you have to ask whether you are an entrepreneur, you are probably not. Entrepreneurship is not a title that someone assigns you; it is a feeling from within. Oftentimes, you may not even know from where that feeling stems, but you know it is there and it cannot be ignored. Entrepreneurship, if you would like to do it in a way that helps you reach your personal level of success and freedom, is no game. Sure, it may look easy and glamorous because of social media photos and strategically captured video stories, but those of us who have survived the hardships and lived to tell about them know differently. If you desire entrepreneurship because it is trendy, do not do it. But if you have that entrepreneurial gut feeling, go for it with everything you have.

Martell

Most people can identify that feeling before taking the leap to entrepreneurship. They recall feeling unsettled. They understand their current work assignment, but they also know that there is more meant for them. Have you felt that way? Right now, you are probably tired of helping others walk their road to wealth while you remain at a stand still. If you have felt that familiar tug, then it is very likely that you are an entrepreneur. I have always worked in one way or another. I started very early mowing lawns for neighbors. Then that led to performing fall leaf clean ups and a cleaning service in college. So entrepreneurship was never far from my mind, regardless of whatever else was happening in my life.

Let me make something clear. If you want to be an entrepreneur, and essentially your own boss because you want to work only when you feel like it; not have to answer to anyone else; or simply for the luxury of designing your own hours, then you do not really want to be an entrepreneur. You are in love with the *idea* of entrepreneurship. Somehow, there is a fallacy that being an entrepreneur is about never having to answer to anyone else, but that could not be further from the truth. If you want to excel and prosper in entrepreneurship, there is always someone else to which you will have to answer – namely, your customer.

It is also important to understand that while you are working for someone else, you should treat that business as if it were your own. Working hard for someone else prepares you to work even harder for yourself. Do not be misled and think that once you become a full-time entrepreneur you will automatically have a change in mindset; you will not. A stellar work ethic is developed over time through practice and dedication. If you will not do it for someone else, you will not do it for yourself. We believe that we have been able to achieve a certain level of success because our strong work ethic was already present and prevalent.

Melody

Social media and serial networking may give the allusion that entrepreneurship is all glitz and glamour, but it is far from that. Entrepreneurship entails early mornings and late nights, client meetings, managing employees, and more customer acquisition in between. There are also some basic traits that any entrepreneur needs to have in his or her toolkit. You may want to perform a *really* honest self-check to determine whether you hold these traits or not.

Because you do not technically have a boss, there is no time clock to hit. There is no one to tell you what needs to be done and there is definitely no one who will stand over your shoulder to make sure you have accomplished the tasks needed to keep your business afloat. Being *self-motivated* is going to be your key asset both in the good and bad times in your business. Be honest with yourself and assess your level of self-motivation.

You cannot just say you want to be successful; you have to be *determined* to succeed. Why? In all honesty, you may hear the word "no" often, and you may have doors closed in your face. You may not immediately make the contacts you were hoping to make. Some months may be more profitable than others. You may find that the people who said that they would support you and have your back have changed their minds when you need them most. You will likely find that you have to be creative in making things happen. There is also a possibility that you will lose some of your biggest contracts, clients, or customers. In spite of all of those obstacles, you will have to be determined to be successful. Your determination will be the deciding factor to whether you cave under the pressure or keep going the next day, and the next, until you have reached success.

The word *brave* gets thrown around pretty loosely, but the fact of the matter is that it takes guts to leap into entrepreneurship. Even after you do everything that you possibly can to make the transition smooth, there will still be hiccups along the way. Knowing this and deciding to take the leap anyway will be one of the bravest choices you will make in life. Every day will be a renewal of your bravery to face new challenges. You must pivot when necessary and face the naysayers who hope to see you fail simply because they were not brave enough to take the leap themselves.

If you can take a long, hard look at yourself (or even ask those closest to you) and decide that you exhibit at least these three characteristics, not just when it is convenient, but especially when the pressure is rising, then you may be an entrepreneur.

9-5 Entrepreneur Exercise

Being an entrepreneur takes guts. It also involves taking risks, being mentally strong, and possessing a commitment to move forward even when things get tough (and things will get tough). To see if you are ready, take our *Entrepreneur Readiness Assessment* below. Mark your strengths with a (+) and your weaknesses with an (-). Do your strengths outweigh your weaknesses? If not, there is work for you to do.

____ I am mentally strong

____ I do not mind taking risks

____When things get hard, I tend to give up

____ I rely on others for validation

____ I will work hard when people are watching me

____ I am self-motivated

____ I do not mind starting from the bottom and working my way up

____ I know how to find answers to questions I may have

____ Sometimes, I can behave lazily

____ I rely on others to do things for me that I can do for myself

____ I have a fear of failure

____ I know how to conduct research and find answers

_____To start my own business, I need a partner

_____ I am determined to succeed, even when things get hard

9-5 NOTES

_____
_____
_____
_____
_____
_____
_____
_____
_____
_____
_____
_____
_____
_____
_____
_____
_____
_____
_____
_____
_____
_____
_____
_____
_____
_____
_____
_____
_____

QUESTION # 2
How do I discover my passion?

This specific question is one that we have gotten many times over the years. People seem to automatically link making money with passion. The truth of the matter is that just because you are in a field that you love does not mean you are going to be successful and make money, and vice versa. Having the ability to make money does not mean that you will be doing work that you love.

We leaped into a field which we had never even heard of and had no prior experience. Although this industry has allowed us to make millions, it was not a passion of ours. What we have learned and you will need to learn as well, is that sometimes you have to do things that will enable you to eventually pursue your passions.

Martell

I have always enjoyed spending time encouraging and helping people to discover how to get to the next level. When we began our lawncare business, lawncare was not my passion. I did enjoy being able to see clients happy with our work and I felt a sense of accomplishment because I had a growing business, but that was not my passion.

All too often, it is not about your passion. Not everything has to be about your passion. You will grow to love some things simply because you are putting your all into them and reaping the benefits. You will cradle it like it is your baby, and before you know it, you will discover a true passion. You can be passionate about something and go broke doing it. Whatever you are doing that is helping you to make money will eventually help you to get to your passion as well. Remember, you may not always be able to do what you love when first starting out.

Begin by thinking about your skill sets. Make a list of all of the ways in which you may be able to earn more money by developing a business. Include both things about which you are passionate and those you are not so passionate. Next, of the skills you listed, place a star by the ones that would be most profitable and would allow you to make the most income. Whether those marked with the stars are your passions or not does not matter. Your goal is to start with an initiative that will allow you to grow into your passion and provide for yourself and your family at the same time. So, the answer to the question, "How do I discover my passion?" is this: You discover it by doing the work that needs to be done.

Melody

As a result of the work we have done in the property preservation industry, I began receiving requests to speak about entrepreneurship. I soon discovered how much I loved speaking to encourage, motivate, and pour positivity and hope into the lives of others. I also realized that it was what I loved about teaching. People would often ask me if I missed teaching and my constant reply was that I missed my students.

What I missed most about the students was having the opportunity to help them see that they could reach all of their goals and live all of their dreams. It was important to be an example of someone who was not born with a silver spoon, but who was still able to pursue all of those things for which I had ever hoped. I wanted to be an everyday example to my students that success is not determined by the environment in which you grew up. It did not matter what family they were born into. They had the power to determine who they were and who they wanted to be. Now, I get to share the same empowerment with larger audiences to impact even more people. It had to come full circle, but eventually it became crystal clear. That is my passion. At the age of 22, I could not have been a motivational speaker and expected people to truly hear or accept my words because I did not have enough credibility. Starting a company that became successful in record-breaking time opened the doors for me to be able to operate in my passion. My passion was never to clean dirty toilets, work into the wee hours of the morning, micro manage contractors, and get a few hours of sleep only to repeat the process again the next day. But, those things did get me to the place where I am now able to put more effort into those areas about which I am most passionate.

I recently had a similar conversation with a friend who is talented in several areas and technically all of those areas could be worked into her business model because they are all related. Like most of us, she was more passionate about one service that she offered than she was about all of the others. Her desire was to focus more of her time and effort on building that "passion" service. In doing so, she quickly realized that it was not a service that brought her the greatest and most consistent earnings. I suggested that she continue to offer her passion service, but that it needed to be offered as a supplementary service and not a main service. She would then need to determine which service would bring her the greatest number of clients and earnings and lead with that one instead. In time, with patience and consistency, she would be able to focus more on her passion.

This may be a difficult concept to grasp, especially when many of the so-called experts say, "follow your passion." But, what we know from experience, rather than just talk, is that following your passion may not always be the smartest or most profitable route.

9-5 Entrepreneur Exercise

Although we do not encourage you to rely exclusively on your passion to determine your entrepreneurial path, it does not hurt to understand your passions and skill sets before you get started.

Take a moment to reflect on your passions, natural talents, and skill sets.

I am passionate about:

_____

_____

_____

I can turn it into a business by:

_____

_____

_____

My natural talents are:

_____

_____

_____

I can turn them into a business by:

_____

_____

_____

My skill sets are:

_____

_____

_____

I can turn them into a business by:

9-5 NOTES

QUESTION # 3
How do I turn my side hustle into a full time business?

We are sometimes hesitant to use the word hustle and business in the same sentence. Although the word hustle has been given a positive connotation in recent years, it can sometimes be attributed to someone who is simply looking for a quick come up rather than seeking to build longevity and wealth within their business. For that reason, we try to encourage people to change their perspectives. We challenge you to think of your company as a business, not a hustle, so that your mindset will be on building wealth versus making money. With that being said, having the desire to turn your "side hustle" into a full-time business is the first step.

Martell

The second step is to legitimize your business. That means that you start with simple processes like naming your business, setting up a business email, and stream lining your pricing. You also need to build a business presence. Nothing will end a business faster than an inconsistent presence. If you are still working your 9-5, you may find it difficult to balance the demands of your job while building your business. In the beginning, you will be the social media manager, customer service agent, and the sole provider of whatever products or services you are offering. At the very least, you should always return emails and phone calls in a timely manner. Always deliver your products or services on time and with exceptional quality.

Whenever possible, go the extra mile and attempt to exceed expectations. Exceeding expectations will help you build a solid reputation. For a small business or new entrepreneur with a limited marketing budget, reputation is everything. In most instances, your reputation will be what makes or breaks your brand. Think about it. How many times have you not patronized a business because you *heard* that it was unprofessional or that the quality of services were substandard? Do not let that business be your business, and do not let a poor reputation break your brand.

Melody

While you are building your presence, be innovative. Do not do something simply because you see others doing it. When we are asked about how we started our business, we often feel like people are looking for an absolute blue print. There is no blue print. We do know that mimicking others will get you nowhere, fast. What works for one person may not work for you anyway, so you may as well stand out. Standing out could mean that you have to provide an extra service that your competitor does not offer. It may also mean that you provide hand made products whereas your competitor buys in bulk. However, you can differentiate yourself will go a long way in taking your company from a side hustle to a legitimate business.

Because we operate in an industry where our competitors mostly provide the same service, we have been able to stand out by providing exceptional service. We will not leave a site, regardless of the condition in which we found a property when we arrived, until the job is complete. More often than not, we go beyond what would typically have been considered necessary to complete the job. We are sticklers for providing exemplary service. That is our trademark and that is how we have been able to build a reputable business and a positive reputation throughout the industry.

You will need to become an avid reader. Read everything that you can about your specific industry. There are no hidden secrets to establishing and building a credible business. In fact, practically everything you will need to know is just a quick Google search away. There are resources that outline exactly what you will need to jumpstart your business, step-by-step.

If you do not want to be viewed as a side hustler, you cannot act like one. Be professional in all of your business related endeavors, regardless of how large or small. Establish a business presence with business cards, a website, and a dedicated business voicemail. Respond to business messages within 24 hours. If there an area in which you know you are not well equipped, take a class. Professional development classes do not have to be expensive. You will have to do your research, but many are free and your local Chamber of Commerce is a great resource to find the classes that may be most beneficial.

9-5 Entrepreneur Exercise

You are working your side hustle, but you are ready to get things moving full speed. Use this checklist to leverage your side hustle into a full time business.

	Yes	No
I have a website.		
I have business cards.		
I have a business email.		
I have set up a professional voice mail.		
I have a pricing structure.		
I have a system by which to address customer concerns and/or complaints.		
I am able to produce enough products/services to meet customer demand.		
I know whether I need a business license or not.		
If I do need a business license, I have secured one.		

I have researched the differences among company structures.		
I have researched the standards and expectations of my industry.		
I have sought professional development.		
I have considered how I will manage my personal and professional life.		
I have researched my competition and found a way to have a competitive edge.		

9-5 NOTES

_____

_____

_____

_____

_____

_____

_____

_____

_____

_____

_____

_____

_____

_____

_____

_____

_____

QUESTION #4
When do I leave my 9-5?

Whoo. Now this is a tough one. Making the decision to leave your 9-5 is not easy, and it is also not a decision that anyone else can help you make. Fear of the unknown will often cause you to continue working for someone else rather than taking a chance on yourself. Sometimes it really just comes down to knowing when it is time to go. Rarely will that time be because you are angry, tired of working, or you just do not want to answer to anyone else any longer. Those are all the wrong reasons to leave. But, if you have been working on your business, planning for your exit, and you have prayed about it, then you will know when it is time to move.

Martell

Timing is everything. You must be willing to stand still and work hard until your way out arrives. It does not mean that everything has to be perfect in order for you to make the great escape, but it does mean that you should try to make certain concessions before departing.

We once heard someone say that you cannot mix faith with foolishness; and that is a true statement. But, if you and God have decided that it is time for you to make your exit, just make sure that you have wisely put some safe guards in place before you take the leap. You will have family and friends who will question your decision. The last thing you want is to have them knocking you down because you took a leap of faith, were not quite ready, and failed because you were ill prepared.

We did not resign from teaching until our lawn care business was profiting six figures. Our decisions to leave our teaching positions were based on two factors: 1) we could no longer handle the demand of working both full time and growing our business and 2) we were no longer satisfied with teaching because of the mental and physical strains.

Our suggestion is that you should leave your 9-5 only once you are stable enough mentally and financially to do so. You should have at least eight months salary saved for living expenses and cushion without depending on your business. If your business has not made it to the point where it completely replaces your former income, I would even suggest that you have a full year of living expenses saved. You can never be too careful or plan too much. Even still, there will be risks involved, which often is just a part of entrepreneurship.

Entrepreneurship has its highs and lows. When business is great, it is easy to be excited. But the excitement can quickly wane when there is not enough money or clients to go around. Then what? Will you remain as committed in bad times as in good times? Will you be willing to do whatever it takes to get business back on track? If you are not sure, you should definitely think this through. Tough times will arise and you need to know if you will be able to weather the storm.

Melody

Running a business calls for a myriad of skill sets. There is advertising, accounting, administrative duties, and client acquisition, just to name a few. Are you equipped for those roles, and if not, will you know how to access help? Be sure that you take inventory of your skill sets beyond just doing the work that you like to do.

With that said, deciding to take the leap is ultimately a personal choice and you have to be comfortable with your decision, regardless of what anyone else may say or think. If we had gone solely based on where we started, we never could have imagined that we would have been able to achieve the things, personally and professionally, that we have. We did not come from rich families, have trust funds, or attend a top ten college, but we did have strong work ethics and the ability to dream big dreams. Our families were supportive, but just like many of you reading this, they were fractured. We could have allowed that single fact to prevent us from digging deeper and taking risks, but we did not.

Those risks included leaving jobs that others around us may have considered "good jobs" to pursue a career in a far less glamorous industry, which was lawn care. Sometimes you have to go against what everybody else is saying to reach your full potential. We did, and we do not regret it. What is holding you back or making you remain in a job where you know there is no room for advancement? What is causing you to continue to grow someone else's dream while yours is put aside? Is it fear of the uncertain or lack of support? You must keep in mind that your growth will always be left in the hands of someone else unless you take control of your life. Face your fears head on, and then get ready to move along.

Let go of societal and familial expectations of what you should be doing to earn a living and find professional happiness. Think about what you want. Think about what would make you happy. Imagine what it would look like. There is no specific picture of success. You have to paint your own.

9-5 Entrepreneur Exercise

Are you interested in entrepreneurship but feel as if your current circumstance may be holding you back? If so, there is nothing left to do but face those circumstances head on. You can start facing those fears now. In the appropriate spaces below, list things that are holding you back, and then list the tiny steps you can take to move them out of your way. Writing down those barriers will be the beginning of helping you to identify them and knock them down, one by one. Having a plan of action against them, no matter how small, is always a step in the right direction.

Ask yourself, "What are some of my fears?" (i.e. fear of failure or fear that my family and friends won't support me?)

_____

_____

_____

_____

_____

_____

_____

_____

_____

_____

_____

_____

_____

_____

_____

What issues are holding me back? (i.e. not having the money to start a business or not having a college degree)

_____

_____

_____

_____

_____

_____

_____

_____

_____

_____

_____

_____

_____

_____

_____

What can I start doing today to face my fears and let go of what is holding me back? (i.e. get a second job to earn more money, complete college applications)

_____

_____

_____

_____

_____

_____

_____

_____

_____

_____

_____

_____

_____

9-5 NOTES

QUESTION # 5
Should I get a bank loan to start my business?

Many people fail to start their businesses because of a lack of money. The good news for most entrepreneurs is that you do not need tons of money to start a business. You simply have to take calculated steps and watch where and how you spend money in your business.

Martell

We started our business with our own money. Because we were still teaching, we used money from our teacher incomes to maintain our household and get the business running. Although most people assume that they can simply go out and apply for a business loan, this is not usually the case. For the most part, you have to be an operable and profitable business before the bank will even consider giving you a business loan. They need to know that you will be able to repay the loan according to their terms. If you are just starting out, have no clients, no business income, and no profit there is no way for you to guarantee that you will be able to repay. Above all else, banks want to protect themselves.

If you really want to get your business started, you will just have to get creative. You can save money from your current income or borrow or ask for monetary gifts from family and friends to jumpstart your business. You can also think of other talents from which you can earn money to start your business. Do not think that because you lack funds you cannot start your business. If you research the stories of some of the world's greatest entrepreneurs, you will find that they did not have much money either. A great majority of them actually borrowed money from friends and family and even ended up in mounds of debt starting their businesses. But, because they were determined to see their dreams come to fruition, they kept moving.

Another point to consider is that even though you may not be able to start your business at the magnitude of which you have dreamed, it is important that you get started. Do not allow money, or the lack thereof, to keep you from moving forward with a plan of action. Plan for what you can do now, and plan for what you would like to be able to do later. Determine how much money you will really need to get started rather than lamenting over how much you think you will need. Do your research, set realistic priorities, and address each one as necessary.

Melody

Most entrepreneurs, especially those who are offering a service rather than a product, do not actually need as much money as they think to start a business. Of course there are exceptions, but if you are not opening a restaurant, a physical retail location, have an immediate need for office space, or require expensive equipment, there are ways to keep your starting costs low.

Also, keep in mind that there are ways to get what you need for less cost. For instance, if you feel you need basic branding like a logo to get started, utilize services like Fiverr to get what you need until you can upgrade (if you decide to do so) later. If you are in need of a website, there are a myriad of resources that make it really easy to build your own. When we first started out, we did not have the luxury of paying someone to build our website, but we needed one. Rather than sulk about not being able to hire a web designer for the job, I built our first website. It was not my favorite task to complete, but when you are starting a business on a super tight budget, you quickly learn how to put your natural talents and skill sets to use.

Also, do not be afraid to ask for favors and help from those around you. Let them know what you need and what you are able to afford. Do not make people feel pressured to help you, but instead make your needs known and be open to accepting assistance in the way that family and friends feel most capable of helping.

9-5 Entrepreneur Exercise

Sometimes we react to a problem before we even have a complete scope of what we need. So, before you claim that you do not have enough money to start your business, take a realistic look at how much money you are really going to need. We have identified some needs that are common among most entrepreneurs and left some space for you to include those specific to your industry. Once you have completed the list, prioritize your needs and work towards addressing them every day.

Basic Expenses	Cost	Industry Expenses	Cost
Logo	$		$
Website	$		$
Business Cards	$		$
Computer	$		$
	$		$
	$		$
TOTAL	$	**TOTAL**	$

9-5 NOTES

QUESTION # 6

What if my family and friends are not supportive?

When you make the decision to leave your 9-5 and pursue your vision and dreams, you will have to understand that everyone will not comprehend your desire for more. But remember, they do not have to comprehend your vision because it does not belong to them.

We earned degrees in education and for the most part, teachers are held in high regard. When we were both teaching and growing our business simultaneously, no one had anything to say. In fact, most of our family and friends were very proud of us. That changed the moment we decided to leave the classroom. They then began to question whether we were making the right decision. They wondered how we would survive, financially. They inquired about how we would maintain our health insurance. Naively, we did not understand why they were not more supportive. We thought it was clear that our business was doing well. They saw us take family vacations and make some of the purchases that we had always wanted to make. Did they really think that we would be able to purchase those things on our teacher salaries alone? Regardless of those facts, we thought they were simply supposed to be supportive because they were our family and friends. Unfortunately, we learned that was not the case. Sometimes it is the people who are closest to you who give you the most grief about your decisions. Most of the time, they do not mean any harm. They simply do not understand, and that is okay. You must forge ahead anyway.

Martell

I cannot say that I was prepared for how quickly our business started to grow, but I was thankful that we were consistently presented with new opportunities, financially and professionally. Growth calls for more of everything. It required more equipment, employees and networking. Essentially, it also brought along more problems. I know that people think money solves problems, but it does not. Money allows you to have more options, but it definitely creates more problems than it solves.

The more success we acquired, the more friends and family we lost. That is one of those things nobody warns you about in building a successful business. It is going to happen, so get ready. Read the stories of entrepreneurs, and they will likely tell you how lonely it can be. You will have to set boundaries and people will not like that. You will have to cut some associations and people will not like that. You will have to place yourself and your business first and people will not like that. Take note of who finds fault in your desire for excellence and do not worry when they exit your life. Consider it a favor.

Honestly, adopting that mentality is much easier said than done. Initially, I helped my family and friends because that is what I wanted to do. Eventually, people around me started to view it as an obligation; they expected unlimited handouts. Because I was in a position to help, I did.

Over the course of time, we were able to hire family members. We figured we needed the workers and they needed the employment, so why not give them a chance. Sadly, as anyone may have been able to predict, hiring them mostly turned out badly. The bottom line is that they expected to be treated like family rather than employees. Some wanted to be paid above industry standard pricing due to the family connection. Others did not like the idea that they were working for us, and instead wanted to treat our business relationship like a partnership. It can be a challenge when you are hiring people who have in the past been the ones from which you may have gotten work or knowledge. Unfortunately, sometimes it is difficult in such cases for those individuals to be content with working for you. Instead, they see you as the same little cousin or little nephew that they saw growing up.

As if dealing with those issues were not enough, we have had family members steal expensive equipment and lie about it once confronted. Eventually we had to install cameras, but that did not stop the theft. I once caught a cousin, red handed, stealing on camera. When questioned about it, he admitted to having stolen the equipment and also admitted to having sold it. Still, I allowed him to continue working.

Some people have asked me if these incidents caused me to harbor any ill will towards my family and friends or maybe regret the decisions that I have made. The answer is always no. I do not allow the actions of others to hurt me or alter my character. My decision has always been based on a desire to help those around me and to offer them opportunities as a result of the ones I have been blessed to have. At the end of the day, I know that I have treated everyone more than fairly, and I find comfort in that. Ultimately, you do have to be just as careful about the friends and family you hire as you do strangers. I am no longer willing to hire a friend or family member just because they are in a tough spot and need a job. I weigh my choices much more carefully now.

In spite of what may seem like a laundry list of downfalls from growing a successful business, they are just part of the territory and in no way detract from the greatness that the business has afforded Melody and I in our lives. I know many people would assume that what I am most proud of is the financial success. To be honest, that is secondary. I am most proud of knowing that this is what God has aligned for my family as long as I followed His instructions. We took a big leap of faith by leaving our secure positions in education. Everything that has happened, even Melody and I meeting and marrying, was all according to His plan for our lives.

Of course we enjoy the financial freedom, but not because we are able to purchase material items, but because we are able to provide our kids with a great education and expose them to things that we could have only imagined. We also feel blessed to be able to create jobs in our community and contribute to causes in which we believe. This has led us to embrace and hold dearly the responsibility to be positive role models for others. We have people who seek us out for advice and guidance. We can only provide them with quality, possibly life altering words if we first seek God. We are thankful and we know that the more thankful we are, the more He will bring our way.

Melody

The loss of friendship can be sudden, brutal and leave you wondering what went wrong. Martell and I both hold our friendships in very high regard. When we form a bond of friendship, we do so with the intentions of it being long lasting. We are also willing to lend a helping hand, when and where we can. So, it is no surprise that loss of friendships, or what we thought were friendships, was a tough pill to swallow. Eventually, you have to accept the reality of who people are or who they have become and continue to move forward.

Another downside to growing a business is that I rarely get to spend time with friends and family. Even while in college, I was not a party girl and preferred spending quality time with quality people. I have definitely missed out on some girlfriend time because of my commitment to work. I think one of the greatest casualties of my work life is missing the relationship with one of my closest aunts. Although she is about fifteen years older than I am, we were more like sisters. She was the person I made late night calls to during college. She would send me spending money so that I could hang out with friends and be able to enjoy my college experience without worrying about how to fund it. I would talk to her nearly every day and see her every chance I could. But with the demands of work increasing year after year, our time together became shorter and further apart. Even when I do get to see her, I am often too tired to chat like old times.

I had to learn quickly and accept that those things come with the territory. When you are an entrepreneur, so much of your time gets dedicated to growing the business and thinking about new opportunities to pursue. We could have never predicted these changes, but doubt our journey would have been the same without them. That is not to give the impression that running a successful business is all doom and gloom, because it is not. For instance, when I think about what I am most proud of in the years we have spent in business, I would have to say that it is the fact that I have not allowed obstacles to hinder me from always striving to be and give my best. Every day is a conscious decision not to give up. I do not give up because my family depends on me, and my employees' families depend on me. In life, we may often wonder why one person is able to do something that the next is not. The fact of the matter is that, at least according to my beliefs, we were not all meant to have the same goals and dreams or live the same life. How boring and bland would that be? Each person has a role that they were created to fill, and I definitely feel that I am playing the one for which I was destined. I could not have ever imagined that a girl like me who grew up in a trailer, sometimes with no running water, in a super small town with one stoplight, would be able to accomplish what I have. But I was able to do it and there are many, many others who can as well.

Another upside to being an entrepreneur and business owner is the ability to live life on my terms. I value the flexibility of being able to tend to my kids' needs when mother duty calls and being able to answer work emails from Cancun. While a vacation in another country can be amazing, I must admit that as an entrepreneur, you are never able to be completely off or detached from work. You are not able to live a normal life. There is no clocking out at five. No matter how much you may believe that because you have staff to rely on you will be able to enjoy some normalcy, you will not. There will always be people depending on you and you will always have to answer the call because at the end of the day, it is your business and your responsibility. Even still there is an undeniable freedom that comes with working for yourself and I would not trade it for the world.

9-5 Entrepreneur Exercise

Before you take the leap, it is great to be mentally prepared for who in your circle might support you and who might present opposition. This will allow you to prepare for how you will deal with their feedback, whether it is negative or positive.

Which family members or friends have you told about your desire for entrepreneurship?

_____
_____
_____
_____
_____

Which family members or friends might invest in your business?

_____
_____
_____
_____
_____

Who do you think would be the most supportive of your business? In what ways will you need their support?

_____
_____
_____
_____
_____

Who do you think would be the least supportive of your business? How can you ensure that they don't have a negative effect on your mindset?

_____
_____
_____
_____
_____
_____
_____
_____
_____
_____
_____
_____
_____

How will you handle it if you do not receive any support from family and friends? Remember support is great, but the lack of it should not deter you from pursuing your dreams and goals.

_____
_____
_____
_____
_____
_____
_____
_____
_____
_____
_____
_____
_____

9-5 NOTES

QUESTION # 7
How do I grow my business?

Business growth does not happen just because you want it. You must have a plan, be very active, and be consistent. Doing half the work, half the time will get you less than half the clients you want, and no growth. If you want to grow your business, roll up your sleeves and be prepared to get dirty.

Martell

In addition to being prepared to get dirty, you have to be strategic. We learned very quickly, that strategic growth is super important when it comes to owning a business. Growing too quickly before you have the necessary procedures and policies in place can break you. Because we were hungry for success, we jumped on numerous opportunities that seemed like a good deal. If challenges arose, we convinced ourselves that we would figure them out along the way. Our first opportunity for growth was in January 2011, when we decided to work directly with a HUD approved Mortgage Field Servicer. When we began in the property preservation industry, we started by shadowing someone who was already experienced in the field. By 2011, after only three months of shadowing, we decided we were ready and equipped to take on more work on our own. We knew that having a direct contract would require more work, but we did not know exactly how much more it would require. Our client quickly began requesting that we go into other areas that included Mobile and Birmingham. At that time, we had only been working the Huntsville area. Always up for a challenge, we jumped at the opportunity. We appreciated the fact that our new client trusted us enough to offer us the chance to expand our territories. We knew it was because of the quality of work we were able to consistently provide.

Before we got to that point, we had grown our lawn care business through more traditional methods. Whether you are in business as a sole proprietor or you have a have partner, you will have to play more than a single role in growing your business. For Melody and me, that meant that we were not only responsible for completing the jobs for which we were hired, but we were also responsible for acquiring new clients and marketing to get them. You will quickly learn that in most industries, clients are not knocking down doors to get to you; instead you have to go out and find them.

One very pivotal way that we did so was door-to-door marketing. We created flyers and would visit all of the houses in a neighborhood, leave our promo materials in the door along with a quote for our services. Our flyers were not produced and printed professionally. Instead, we created them on our computer and made copies for distribution right at home. After school hours and on the weekends, we would canvas neighborhood after neighborhood for several consecutive days. Although this strategy may sound intimidating, exhaustive, or even old fashioned, it worked. We were able to gain over 50 residential clients within a few months. From there, we were able to garner more word of mouth and our clientele steadily increased. We did not spend money on ads or billboards and focused on what had proven to work, which was simple business cards and made from home flyers.

Of course, it was not easy, but no worthwhile work is ever easy. That set the standard for how hard we were willing to work for our success and that has been with us until this day.

Melody

When you are growing your business, sweat equity is imperative because it teaches you everything you need to know about the entire operation of your company. Building your company brand the right way will only happen if you are actively involved in the entire process. We had no idea that part of the job would include cleaning dirty toilets, or work in properties with no air, electricity or running water. What we *did* know was that we were working to build our brand and laying the foundation for something great. We knew that before we could walk we had to crawl.

Eventually, we began running. Before we knew it, we had taken on three additional clients to service their bank-owned inventory. We were not only covering the entire state of Alabama, but we had expanded into Mississippi and Tennessee as well. Honestly, it was a little scary at first. Covering three states was definitely not something that we could handle on our own, so we had to make sure we had people in place before we agreed to service those areas. That was part of our strategy.

What was also part of our strategy, and it should be yours too, was to be visible. Unless you are catering to invisible customers, you do not need to have an invisible brand. No one can enlist your services if they do not know that you exist. Being visible means that you are in tune with the channels that are relevant to your industry. In addition to your website, you should make your brand visible on LinkedIn, Facebook, and Instagram. Your industry and the type of customer you are after will determine the social media platform that will be most beneficial to you. A simple Google search will help you determine a great deal of this information. Do not be shy about self-promotion. If you do not speak up on behalf of your business, who will? Refine your elevator pitch and be prepared to give it at the drop of a dime. The more invested and familiar you are with your business, and what you have to offer, the more you will attract the business acquaintances and customers that you are after.

9-5 Entrepreneur Exercise

Whether you are an established business owner, a newbie, or simply considering what product or service you have to offer through business, your goal should be to deliver exceptional service that sets you apart from the crowd. Remember that there are very few new ideas so there is no need to reinvent the wheel, but your goal is to stand out. Brainstorm below on how you can do so.

Describe your (potential) product or service.

_____

_____

_____

_____

_____

Think of your competitors, both locally and nationally. What do they do to attract customers?

_____

_____

_____

_____

_____

Now, what can you do differently or what sets you apart?

_____

_____

_____

_____

_____

9-5 NOTES

_____
_____
_____
_____
_____
_____
_____
_____
_____
_____
_____
_____
_____
_____
_____
_____
_____
_____
_____
_____
_____
_____
_____
_____
_____
_____
_____
_____
_____
_____
_____
_____

QUESTION # 8

Should I attend networking events to grow my business?

We have a saying and it is, "Network to build your net worth." Networking is absolutely important and it should begin long before you leave your 9-5. That is how you build relationships, find potential clients, form business partnerships, and learn about what is happening in your community. But all networking events are not created equal. Just like growing your business should be strategic, so should your networking. We all know people who attend every networking event in town, hand out fifty business cards, talk non-stop about themselves, but rarely land a new client or more business. That is because they are networking the wrong way. We want to help you network the right way.

Martell

Networking starts before you leave your 9-5 job. If you wait until after you leave your 9-5 to start networking and building relationships, you will already be behind the curve. Once you have made the decision that entrepreneurship is in your future, you need to act accordingly. You should begin by researching professional organizations within your industry. If they offer open meetings, visit them a few times to see if they are worth your time. Should you find that they are, join them. Identify where your potential customers are located and visit those places. Initiate relationships with your competitors. This may sound counterintuitive, but it is actually very smart. Competition does not have to be ugly, especially when your competition has been around longer or if they serve a particular niche. You will be able to learn something from them. Let friends and family know that you actually have a business. If they do not need your services, they may be able to refer you to people who do. Remember to be of service to others rather than constantly trying to sell them your products or services. Nobody likes a pushy salesman, but everyone loves a genuine helper.

Pay close attention to the type of networking event you plan on possibly attending. Unfortunately, not all networking events are created equally. Some of them fill up with entrepreneurs and business owners looking to make genuine connections. Others run over with entrepreneurs and business owners who are simply looking to make a sale. There are others who have given as much thought to their overall business growth as a three-year-old has given to their college of choice; they are basically just there for the food and drinks. You want to be around like-minded people who are seeking genuine connections because you know that is one of the keys to success. In the beginning, you may choose to attend every event that runs across your Facebook timeline, and that is okay because you do not know which are beneficial until you have tried a few. Eventually, you should understand the events that will work in your favor. Generally speaking, any networking event attracts a certain demographic of people. You have to decide if those people are the people you would like to get to know. If they are, great; continue visiting. If not, ditch them and move on to the next event. Attend networking events designed especially for your industry, and if you can, seek out other, more established experts in your industry who might allow you to shadow them. As an entrepreneur, especially one who is still working a 9-5, your time is too valuable to waste, even for an hour or two, at an event that does not serve your overall goal.

Have a plan. Because your time is valuable and you want to make the most of every opportunity, never attend a networking event without a plan. It can be as simple as deciding that you would like to meet one person so that you can follow up with him or her after the event or there may be someone attending whom you have been wanting to meet. Your goal then becomes to introduce yourself to that individual or, better yet, have a mutual acquaintance make the introduction. You should also know that some event registration pages allow attendees to see the names of those who have registered to attend. Use that list to your advantage. If you are not sure if the person you would like to meet will be there, consider some other benefit from attending. If attending does not bring you value, regardless of how large or small, stay home. You can use that time to work on your business.

Melody

Listen more than you speak. When you do speak, ask questions. After you have gotten a few networking events under your belt, you will soon have learned that for most people their greatest topic of interest is themselves. As a savvy entrepreneur, you will learn to use that bit of information to your advantage. Learning to be an active listener will become one of your greatest networking skills. People will usually tell you everything you want to know, and then some, if you will only give them the opportunity to speak. Most of us are so eager for our chance to speak, that we do not hear anything. Stop that and start listening. Pay attention to what people need in their own businesses and who they would like to meet. Learn their pain points and then figure out how you might be able to serve them. That is how relationships are formed and how clients are gained. Do not be afraid to ask relevant questions. If there is something you would like to know, and it is not in poor taste or disrespectful to ask, then by all means ask away. Remember, we all like talking about ourselves and sharing our expertise. It is more likely than not that the person to whom you are speaking will be more than willing to answer your questions.

Save your business cards. Do not shove your business card into the hands of every person you meet. If people want to remain in contact, they will ask for a card. Forcing a business card upon them only ensures that your card will end up in a nearby trash bin.

If your networking is not increasing your net worth, you may be doing something wrong. Revisit your networking strategy and access where you may be able to make changes. Do you need to attend a new set of events? Should you be attempting to meet another set of people. Are you doing more talking than listening? Only you will be able to identify exactly what needs to be tweaked and why, but understanding that there is an art to networking and following the steps above are a great start.

9-5 Entrepreneur Exercise

We want you to network in a way that is beneficial to you and your business. That means you need to focus on the quality of your networking events rather than networking for quantity. The next time you're gearing up to attend an event, ask yourself the following questions.

If you end up with more "no" answers than "yes" answers, stay home.

QUESTION	ANSWER
Is the structure of the networking event beneficial to my type of business?	
Will I have the opportunity to meet/speak with people of interest?	
Is there a cost for the event? If so, does the potential to meet like-minded people outweigh the cost of attendance?	
Am I prepared to attend the event? (i.e. you have worked on your elevator pitch; you have business cards and/or other promotional representation of your business)	

Will I commit to meeting and following up with at least one person at the event?	

9-5 NOTES

_____
_____
_____
_____
_____
_____
_____
_____
_____
_____
_____
_____
_____
_____
_____
_____
_____
_____
_____
_____
_____
_____
_____
_____
_____
_____
_____
_____
_____

QUESTION #9
When do I hire help?

Martell

When you begin your business, it is common to feel that you can do everything, and in the beginning you probably can. Because we started our business with our own money and made every effort not to apply for business loans, we actually did take care of all business related tasks ourselves. During the day we would work our 9-5's, and at night we would process orders. Eventually, we became overwhelmed and handling everything began to take both a physical and mental toll. We knew it was time to hire help when we could no longer keep up with client requests. When you know, without a doubt, that you are getting up and making the most of every hour, and you still cannot keep up, you need help. Each day, we would leave home at five in the morning, return at seven at night, and begin uploading and closing out orders. We would get a few hours of sleep and awake to do the same thing over again the next day. We desperately needed more team members.

After realizing that having to process orders everyday did not allow us to fully operate in the best interest of our growing business, we decided to hire someone to process the orders completed throughout the day. That was one of the best decisions we made. We did not have all of the systems and processes figured out before we made the hire. We did not even have office space at that time, but we saw the bigger picture. We knew what having an employee would provide for us and how it would allow our business to continue to flourish. So we made our first hire and that employee was able to work from home. Sure, we would have loved to have office space before bringing someone on the team as that does bring about a certain level of legitimacy. But again, everything will not always unfold the way society makes you feel it is supposed to unfold.

Knowing when to hire help is a determination you will have to make without input from anyone else. These are some clear signs that you might need help:

If you:

- Find yourself dedicating 15 or more hours per day to completing business work tasks.

- Are no longer able to meet your current clients' expectations.

- Are no longer able to take on new clients.

- Are afraid to expand or grow because you are not sure you can handle the work load.

Not growing because you do not have enough people on your team should never be a problem. You cannot get to the next level if you do not invest back into your company, and sometimes this means hiring help. We have seen countless companies fail because the owners want to pocket more money instead of investing in their businesses, and as a result, they begin to lose customers and clients. Think about the last time you visited a small business in an effort to support, and you were on hold too long or you had to wait too long to receive your food. If you are like most people, you likely decided to take your business elsewhere. Those are pitfalls you want to avoid and many times they can be avoided by ensuring you have enough of the right help on your team.

Melody

Although you certainly need the right help on your team, do not take hiring employees lightly, especially if you decide to fill a full-time position. It is one thing to feel the responsibility and pressure of providing for your own family and doing what it takes to make that happen. However, it is quite another to also carry the weight of providing for another family, because as an employer, that is essentially what you are doing. Think about your business growth and how consistent it has been and make a calculated (not hopeful) projection on its future growth. Once you have considered those factors and are ready to move forward, you will need to get clear on whom you need to hire.

It is rare that you would need someone who brings exactly the same set of skills to the table that you already have. Consider the range of tasks that need completing in order for your business to run successfully. Which of those are you able to handle without neglecting the business itself? Once those tasks have been identified, then you will know for which tasks you will need to hire.

You also need to be clear on what you want in an employee. Rather than hiring strictly based on a list of qualifications, think about who would be the best fit outside of obvious criteria like academic credentials and experience. For instance, if you are hiring someone for marketing, you may want to ensure that they not only have a background in marketing, but that they also have the personality suited for marketing tasks like cold phone calls or cold visits. If you will need someone who can work later in the evenings and on weekends, you will need to understand whether your potential hire is really able to do so (and not just saying so for the sake of the interview). Unless you would like to do a boatload of hand holding after the training period is up, consider whether the person you are hiring is a self-starter.

The clearer you are on your needs before you send out the advertisement for help, the better off you will be in the long term.

9-5 Entrepreneur Exercise

Is it really time for you to hire help? Let's find out. Track your work time and activities for five full business days. At the end of the week, answer the following questions. If you answer "yes" to three or more questions, it may be time to hire.

- Did you find yourself dedicating 15 or more hours per day to completing business work tasks?

- Did you find yourself falling short in meeting some client expectations?

- Were you unable to take on new clients?

- Did you find yourself wishing, on more than one occasion, you had help?

- Did you, at any point, find yourself relying on friends or family members to help you meet client and business obligations?

9-5 NOTES

QUESTION # 10

How can I balance the challenge of taking care of my family and growing a business?

It is difficult to present and summarize all of the challenges we have faced as business owners and parents. Learning to balance and excel is difficult. But it can be done. It is important to support each other, and if you can find a quality support system, that is even better. The fact of the matter, however, is that the responsibilities of growing a business and raising a family will fall on you and you alone. That is why it is important that you not only make time for each other, but yourself as well. Being overwhelmed, constantly tired, and stretched thinly does no good for anyone, especially the family. There is no room to give to anyone or anything else if you have first not made the time for yourself. Also, you will often find that men and women decompress very differently. Give your spouse or partner the space required to reload. In the long run, it will be more rewarding and beneficial for the business, and most importantly, the family.

Martell

In 2011, after the tornadoes hit Huntsville and destroyed our home, we packed up our belongings that remained and, for the first time, moved away from our family and friends. We had been considering the possibility of leaving Alabama and exploring new opportunities in a new city, so in the wake of the tornados we decided that there was no better time than the present. Excited about the chance to start over and maybe doing something more, we put our fears of being away from home, as a new couple and business owners, behind us.

But, we were immediately jolted back to reality. A week after settling in Florida, we found out Melody was pregnant with our first child. To say that I was excited would be the understatement of the century. But, underneath the excitement was a bit of apprehension. We would be first time parents raising a child and growing a business. Our support systems were miles away and we were not quite sure how we felt about starting our family, without family around. Even though those lingering doubts were always in the background, I was ecstatic about my wife's pregnancy. I had no fears about becoming a father because I knew I would be great. The absence of my own father did not cause me to doubt myself. If anything, it helped me to know that I could, and would, be better to my own children.

I felt even more secure in the fact that we had been steadily working and growing our business so we were in a pretty decent financial position as soon-to-be parents. All of our hard work was paying off and had led to us starting our family comfortably. But no financial comfortability could compensate for the fact that Melody was lonely and, very often, ill. The pregnancy, though still early, was taking a toll on her, physically and mentally. Because we were both feeling the sting of being away from family, we decided after living in Florida for three months, to move back to Alabama. It was a simple decision really. We wanted to be around family and friends during this time. Melody, understandably, wanted to be closer to her mom. It took nothing away from our ambitions or the business to make the move home. In fact, the longer we were away the more we realized that not only did we need to be back home to be with our family, but we also needed to be there for the sake of our business.

After our daughter was born later that year, I was on cloud nine. Although I was out working, I tried my best to ease Melody's load and be active, especially in the early months. Of course, it probably was not enough to give her the adequate time needed to adjust to having a new baby at home and working, but I did the best I could at the time. No matter how much you look forward to the arrival of a newborn you can never be completely prepared.

Even as we made adjustments at home, we had to continually make them in our business. We were in search of a new office space, a new administrative assistant, and more workers to cover the growing demand. I seemed to be needed more and more in the field and that definitely detracted from my time at home. I look at it now as having made a sacrifice so that I could be more present later. I would not say that it ever really gets easier, especially if you have a desire for continued growth, but you do learn to become better at balancing everything on your plate.

Melody

I have always loved kids, and had often said that I wanted to have at least four of my own. So, when I learned I was pregnant with my first child I could not have been happier. The only damper on my mood was the fact that we had just moved away from Alabama to Florida, and I would be away from my mom. I think most women look forward to being able to share their first pregnancy with their mothers and feeling as if I would not be able to do so really did steal a bit of my pregnancy joy. Couple that with the fact that my morning sickness was unlike anything I had ever imagined and it was easy to understand how my feelings of excitement would swing, like a crazy pendulum, to feelings of being overwhelmed.

Thankfully, my husband was perceptive and quickly picked up on my mood and the affect it was having on my pregnancy. I do not think I ever packed as fast in my entire life as I did when he suggested that we head back to Alabama. Being home allowed me to enjoy and relish my pregnancy. The overwhelming feeling subsided and I was able to focus more on taking care of myself, delivering a healthy baby girl, and working to grow the business. I worked just as long and hard during my pregnancy as I had beforehand. One thing about entrepreneurship is it does not stop because you want to take a break. No matter how much it appeared to others that I needed to slow down, I knew my body and my limits. The baby and I were healthy, I was eating well, and continuing to work certainly did more good for me than harm. I literally worked up to the time of my delivery.

In January 2012, our beautiful baby girl, Mariah, was born. I was glad to be starting my new journey as a mother, but it was difficult for me to abandon work mode. While still in the hospital bed, I was asking for my laptop, responding to clients, and quelling employee fires. I did not neglect my newborn at all, but I learned very quickly to multi-task. At that time, we had not decided on an office space and the young ladies we considered hiring to offer administrative assistance just did not work out. I was not able to delegate those tasks to anyone while I recovered from my pregnancy and bonded with my child, so I had to handle them myself. To me, it was simply par for the business course.

While it was business as usual, I soon found it difficult adjusting to caring for my baby. The constant nursing, diaper changing, and crying did nothing to help the growing lack of sleep I was facing. I began to wonder whether all new mothers faced these challenges. I looked forward to visitors because at least during that time, there was someone around to share the load, even if it was temporary. Martell was helpful, and very hands-on, but he could not neglect his commitment to our business to stay home with me. Looking back, I think I may have suffered a bit from postpartum depression, but how could I have really known? Nobody had mentioned that it was a possibility. No one had given me any warning signs to keep an eye out for. Everything I ever heard or read suggested that the bond between a new mother and child was miraculous and instant. However, it was not that way for me. Eventually, through trial and error, and much prayer, I was able to get a firm, steady grasp on motherhood.

By the time Mariah was about three months old, I started to feel like a pro. We had both gotten settled into a schedule, we were sleeping a bit better, and I found a better balance between work and home. But, I also received the shock of the year. I was pregnant with our second child. Although, it was a surprise, it was a welcomed one. Martell and I had always discussed having our children grow up together, close in age. Because I grew up as an only child, I did not want my child to suffer the same fate. The timing may have been off by a year or so, but I still looked forward to the birth of our second child in December of 2012, Martell II. The transition from a mother of one to a mother of two was much easier than my first go around. I felt more confident in my ability to manage home and business.

We welcomed our third child, Maliah, in February of 2016. By that point, I had figured out the details of how to manage work and family, at least as much as anyone really can. I am probably like most moms and not as overbearing as I was with my first child. I have certainly learned what I should be concerned about versus what things I just need to drop for the sake of my sanity. I make sure to give myself a break when needed. If that means a nap in the middle of the day, and a massage while the kids are at school, or a late night of binge watching Scandal on Netflix, then that is exactly what I will do. I know that in order for me to take care of both my family and my business, I have to be well.

In addition to maintaining my obligation to my children, I have also had to learn how to balance my role as a woman in a male dominated field with my role as a wife. That matters because as a woman in a male dominated industry, I am viewed with a cast of doubt from the outset. Many feel as if I am simply a help to my husband, in the role of the office manager. They fail to realize that I am actually quite a force with which to be reckoned.

It did not take long before I realized that far too often niceties could be misconstrued as weakness. Women in business have to walk a very fine line between being assertive and confident and loud and obnoxious. Whereas men who are confident and outspoken are viewed as leaders, women of the same nature are touted as bossy and over bearing. I learned to be assertive, without seeming aggressive. I learned to speak up for myself and to hold tightly to those things in which I believed. The bolder I grew in business, the bolder I grew in life.

Eventually, that started to become a problem at home. I had to remember that my husband was not one of the men at a job site, or a contractor I was negotiating with over the phone. He was my business partner, and most importantly, the man of the house. To maintain peace and order at home, I had to flip the switch from one place to the next. At the office, I was the boss and not one to be intimidated. At home, I was a wife and mother. I also had to realize that my struggle, like so many others in life, was nothing new.

9-5 Entrepreneur Exercise

There is a very delicate balance between self, family, and business. It is often hard to find, but with intentional focus on what you want for yourself and your family, it can be achieved. Think about ways in which you can set aside time for yourself, your spouse, and your children. Outline them below and come back to the page whenever you, or the family, need a recharge.

To help you out, we have included a sample of some of our favorite activities.

Martell	Melody	Family
Long drives	Massages	Attending church
Reading	Girls' night out	Fun at the lake
Hiking	Netflix	Family cookouts

Now it is you turn:

Yours	Spouse	Family

9-5 NOTES

QUESTION # 11

What else do I need to know about being the boss?

Martell

It is important to note that pursuing entrepreneurship is not about being your own boss, not answering to anyone else, or immediately making tons of money. As long as you have clients, you will have a boss. There is always someone to whom you have to answer. If making money holds more of a priority than working hard, keeping your word, and providing exceptional, professional services, your business may be doomed from the start.

Television and social media can easily make owning and running a business look glamorous and painless, but that depiction could not be further from the truth. Just as much as there is reward in business ownership, there is also failure. Failed relationships, failed partnerships, failed employees…the list literally goes on.

There is also a need to make an impression in your particular field. With hundreds of businesses starting everyday, there are few that are original. We were not the first couple to start a lawn care business and we definitely will not be the last. The difference is what we were able to bring to the table. Because we are both detailed oriented and pride ourselves on professionalism, we were able to offer incomparable levels of quality and service. We expected the same of our employees and when they were not able to deliver, we had to remove them from our realm of business.

This was often difficult because we felt so blessed to help others provide for their families. In order to continue being such a blessing, we needed to continue to be surrounded by a quality team, and you will need to do the same. Entrepreneurship often calls for quick and difficult decision making. However, the more you know the better prepared you will be when you come face to face with obstacles in your path.

Melody

When people put on the "owner" hat, typically they automatically think, 'I'm the boss and I don't have to answer to anyone.' News flash. It does not matter if you are working for someone else or not, you are never truly your own boss. While being a business owner allows for far more flexibility, you must know that you always have someone which to answer. This may be in the form of clients, customers, or vendors, but please know, someone is always holding you accountable. You will have deadlines to meet, meetings to attend, orders to fulfill, or products to ship. In our particular industry, deadlines, and ability or failure to meet them, can either increase or decrease our volume of work and income.

We were once asked about the type of work ethic you must possess to be the boss. When we began to think back on how we performed when we were working for someone else, we remembered that we have always possessed a strong work ethic. We have always been willing to do whatever it takes to get the job done, even when working for someone else. When you are your own boss, no one is going to be standing over you to ensure that you are doing what you need to do to attract business. If you are not a person who is already self-motivated and self-driven, it may be naïve to think that you will start to miraculously possess that level of drive, even when it comes to working for yourself.

You will also need to strengthen your time and stress management skills. There are so many factors that can contribute to running a successful business and many of them will go haywire at any given time. It will happen, and depending on the nature of your business, it may happen often. You will have employees who do not keep their end of the bargain. There will be clients who do not pay their invoices in a timely fashion. You may have clients to cancel orders at the last minute. Sometimes you will just be too tired and overwhelmed to even think straight. But, you will have to pull it together to get the job done, and done right, even if you have to do it all by yourself.

These things are not written to discourage you. Actually, it is quite the opposite actually. I want you to be prepared to face whatever comes your way. Sure, there will be surprises but they do not have to completely throw you off the path you were destined to walk.

9-5 Entrepreneur Exercise

Being the boss means making boss decisions. As glamorous as entrepreneurship may look on social media, the behind the scenes shots usually reveal a different story. We want to help you take a real look at your ability to be the boss. Get honest and give yourself a grade on the boss qualities we have listed below. You know the drill. A grade of "A" means you excel in that area. An "F" means you have got some real work to do.

Start work immediately on improving any areas in which you may fall short.

BOSS QUALITY	A	B	C	D	F
I meet my deadlines.					
I am proactive rather than reactive.					
I am able to receive constructive criticism.					
I operate from a place of character and integrity.					
I already have a solid work ethic.					

9-5 NOTES

QUESTION # 12

Some people say that faith and business are separate, but I am not sure. Do you think faith has played a role in the success of your business?

Martell & Melody

When it comes to our faith and our family, there are no two perspectives because they are one. We know that everything we have been able to accomplish is because God has allowed it to happen. Yes, we were able to dream about where we wanted our business to go and what we would like to have for our family, and we worked towards those things. However, without God it would not have been possible.

Having a foundation of faith is critical. There is no way to have one set of beliefs for your personal life, and another for business. The two paths will cross and if they are not in alignment, there will be trouble. Knowing what you stand for, and what you will and will not do for money, will be one of the greatest attributes in learning to conduct honest business. Our faith and commitment to God has been the center of our marriage and our business. We know that because of Him we have found success in both. In building our faith, family, and business we have adopted three basic principles: pray, listen, and give.

When we say that we consult with God about everything, we mean everything. Our prayer life covers all facets of life from projects to accept, the possibility of expansion, and even which clients with whom to work. God will guide you in business just as He does spiritually. But first, we encourage people to learn how God speaks to them. For some, He may speak through others. He may speak through dreams, or He may speak directly through prayer.

Once you figure that out you need to be ready to listen. So often we ask God to respond to our prayers, but we do not wait around for the answer. You cannot just pray and walk away. You have to be ready and open to listen.

It has also helped us to understand the importance of giving back and serving the communities that have nurtured and grown us. Although we have faced many challenges, the reward has been greater than we could have expected, and for that we are thankful.

9-5 Entrepreneur Exercise

It is time to consider how your values align. At the end of the exercise, you should recognize some sort of correlation among the three. If not, you may have some things to consider.

Below, circle your top five personal values.

abundance   acceptance   beauty   care   money   education
social acceptance   benevolence   security   kindness   love
accomplishment   boldness   being the best   ambition
belonging education   faith   fame   financial independence
family   affluence gratitude   health   honesty   joy   love
independence   intimacy   making a difference   power
practicality

Next, circle your top five faith based values.

gratefulness   kindness   devotion   riches   faith   lightness
joy   insightfulness   introspection   guidance   growth
grace   giving   accountability   diligence   change
challenge receiving   courage   conformity   desire
direction

Lastly, consider, and circle, the top five values you would like to hold in business.

devotion   discipline   fairness   firmness   flexibility
growth   guidance   integrity   leadership   profits   adoration
money   wealth   faith   security   making a difference
partnership   philanthropy   popularity wisdom   reputation

respect   professionalism originality   loyalty   recognition
reliability   teamwork   status   master

9-5 NOTES

_____
_____
_____
_____
_____
_____
_____
_____
_____
_____
_____
_____
_____
_____
_____
_____
_____
_____
_____
_____
_____
_____
_____
_____
_____
_____
_____
_____
_____
_____
_____
_____
_____
_____
_____
_____